THE
PAUSE
for the
Him-Possible

SUSAN HOHMAN

The Pause for the Him-Possible

Cover Design by Susan Hohman & Tim Cummings

Photos courtesy of Canva Designs

Interior design by Susan Hohman

Chapter illustrations courtesy of various copyright-free photo or clip-art sources.

*Attribution for brief quotes, lyrics, or literary references is given directly within the context of the book.

Source of all Scripture quotations in this book are noted.

Printed in the USA

The information presented herein represents the view of the author as of the date of publication.

For information, contact: sushoh@yahoo.com

Dedication

I dedicate this book to my loyal, faithful, and supportive family. Without their unwavering belief in my abilities and constant encouragement, I could never have accomplished the writing of this book.

So very many people have been a part of this journey: my dear late husband, Robert Hohman, Sr.—who believed in me and my talents wholeheartedly, my children: Bobby, Heather, Haleigh, & Collin (and their spouses!)—who give unceasing motivation when I feel my own flagging, my friends—who have always indicated they are my 'fans,' as well as friends, and to my late mother and father, Elsie and Marvin "Whitey" Walton, and my late step-mother, Lesta Ludlow Walton—who would not let me be or achieve less than what they knew I could. This book is dedicated to all of you.

Table of Contents

Preface

As a writer, one of the greatest grammatical assets (and often misused) is the symbol for a pause. A comma, a colon, a semicolon, a period, a dash, a double-dash, or an ellipsis are all grammatical means to express the need to "take a breath" in the reading. The non-use of such marks drives the good reader crazy! He or she feels the need to just keep putting the words together--with no breath, nor without pause. So, consider the difference that little mark can make to the WAY it is read. An entire meaning can be changed by the use of or lack of use of these little pause marks.

My personal favorite is the ellipsis. You know, the . . . thing when you're reading (oft-times referred to as the 'dot, dot, dot'). Some folks think it stands for 'et cetera,' or used to indicate that information is being left out. And, I will concede that it does. But -- to me -- it denotes a holding of the breath in suspense! That may seem a bit fanciful, I suppose. But, I think of it as a nice, suspenseful pause in anticipation of what is coming next! There is something very strategic in the use of a pause: a conscientious building toward an expected -- or even unexpected -- finale!

Isn't that what you want to see when it comes to believing in the miraculous? Your faith is so very important in the realm of the supernatural events you want to see take place. After all, if you could do it yourself, it wouldn't be SUPER-natural. In addition to that faith, however, *I believe that we often need to take time to 'hold our breath' and wait with great anticipation for what is about to happen when we pray for a miracle!*

Most of us know -- and believe -- that God is the God of the impossible. But, did you realize that sometimes we have to back off -- TO PAUSE -- to allow God the freedom to DO the impossible?! In our hurry to see things done, to prod God into "doing His job," sometimes we inhibit His access to the miraculous. You don't believe me? God CAN do anything, but He will rarely follow a plan that you've laid out for yourself. *Your plan stands in the way of His path, and that indicates to Him that you don't need His help.* Ouch.

So, with that in mind, armed with unwavering belief in our limitless God, let us also take time to PAUSE for the HIM-POSSIBLE as we navigate this amazing journey of faith and its rewards!

God bless each of you richly! ~SEH

DAY 1-- Pause to Reset Your Mindset

When considering the concept of believing, one thing resounds over and over — we CHOOSE how and what we believe. Or *not* believe.

I love researching quotes and thoughts of others, because it helps me process my own belief system. The following two quotes were about the month of November in particular:

"No shade, no shine, no butterflies, no bees, no fruits, no flowers, no leaves, no birds — November!" ~Thomas Hood

"In November, the trees are standing all sticks and bones. Without their leaves, how lovely they are, spreading their arms like dancers. They know it is time to be still." ~Cynthia Rylant

One writer saw everything about November as a negative. No, no, NO!

The other saw the month of November as an opportunity to view the beauty around her without a covering, and likened the bare trees to dancers awaiting their next movement!

As I pondered these two opposing views, I grew convinced that my view of a subject or idea is entirely dependent on my MINDSET.

- I know how to be abased, and I know how to abound. Everywhere and in all things I have learned both to be full and to be hungry, both to abound and to suffer need. I can do all things through Christ who strengthens me. ~Philippians 4:12-13 *(NKJV)*

The Apostle Paul realized that he could LEARN how to deal with various situations, by changing his mindset. He knew there would be circumstances that were less than pleasant, but with a change in the way he *looked* at things, he could *do all things*--with Christ's help.

If, with a proliferation of environmental, political, and social uncertainties and abounding turmoil, I choose to look at anything with dread and apprehension, that's what it would become for me. For instance, Negative November: Dreary, unappealing, and full of nothing.

On the other hand, if I choose to face the upcoming unknown as an OPPORTUNITY to PAUSE and watch God do what ONLY He can, it would become an occasion for victories and miracles! I choose NO DOUBTS!

Our mindset, then, is SO important to our outcomes. Is it time for a RESET of your MINDSET?!

For those whose goal is a healthier lifestyle, there is first the necessity of a change in mindset about foods and activity. The consumption of food should be enjoyable. That's why color, style, and presentation is important to the attraction of a meal. A cheeseburger and french fries might taste good and satisfy your cravings, although it is definitely not the healthiest of meals. But, even the most avid fast-food aficionado might be tempted by a plate of colorful lean meats and vegetables seasoned, prepared, and plated to appeal to the palate. *Your mindset, then, can be aided by methods.*

Most people do not go from the couch to running a 5K overnight. Without the proper training and building of stamina to endure, the goal is simply a lofty ideal, and likely not to happen. Instead, it's important to focus on changing one thing at a time. Take a few extra steps each day -- on purpose. Instead of parking as close to a store as possible, choose a spot a little farther away, and gradually work up to more intentional exercise. *Your mindset, then, can be aided by premeditation.*

Now, let us apply these same concepts to our mindset on believing! Do you need a faith-building exercise to keep you spiritually fit? *Do you need to consume less spiritual junk food and seek out the nourishment that will appeal AND fulfill your innermost needs?* Then, I pray that these devotions will be just the impetus that you need.

THE PAUSE

So, for today: Stop. Clear your mind of negative thought patterns and doubt. Push the junk food to the side and make room for the healthy plate of unwavering belief. Make it appealing. Put words of positive belief on it and serve it to yourself frequently throughout your day. "I choose to speak LIFE over this situation." "I CAN do all things through Christ, who strengthens me." "WITH God, all things are possible."

Then, let's PAUSE for the HIM-POSSIBLE as we start our healthy spiritual journey.

DAY 2-- Pause to Believe

- For assuredly, I say to you, whoever says to this mountain, 'Be removed and be cast into the sea,' and does not doubt in his heart, but believes that those things he says will be done, he will have whatever he says.

    ~Mark 11:23 *(NKJV)*

Does NOT doubt ... BUT believes. This scripture is actually an explanation of the one preceding it, "So Jesus answered and said to them, 'Have faith in God'." Apparently He chose to clarify for them exactly what that meant!

Jesus encouraged them to have HIM-POSSIBLE faith! He demonstrated the potential power that comes from NOT doubting, but in believing. Even though it would be their words, quantifying what they wished to happen, it was their faith — unleashed and uninhibited— that would determine the outcome.

15

We have SO many things vying for our attention right now: political uncertainties, unrest among the unruly, natural disasters occurring daily, unknown and seemingly uncontrollable diseases and afflictions, and unstable economic systems, to name but a few.

If we allow them to, they will steal all our time and concern, and keep us from depending FULLY on the ONLY One who controls it all anyway. So, let's lay aside these worries (which do not help us to cope), and let's turn our mindsets on hope.

THE PAUSE

Take time to PAUSE for the Him-Possible today! What mountain do you need moved? Where do you want it to go? What is required of you before it can happen? You must first <u>believe</u>. YOU speak the words—and Do. Not. Doubt.— and watch what GOD will do! *What looked like an unclimbable, impenetrable obstacle will be Him-Possibly removed!!!*

DAY 3-- Pause with Expectancy

My mind moves almost non-stop. My lists are never-ending. My tasks mount up faster than I can accomplish them. One appointment leads to another obligation, until I feel like the proverbial gerbil on the wheel in a cage going nowhere fast! It sometimes feels as though both sleep AND rest are elusive.

So, what IS the answer to coping with all these (mostly) self-inflicted mountains in my life and in yours, too? It's simple. Pause. Stop. Give it a break. Hope, not cope!

- Trust in the LORD with all your heart, And lean not on your own understanding. ~Proverbs 3:5 *(NKJV)*

Two very important instructions contained in this scripture are based on the words, "trust" and "lean."

- First, we are to TRUST in the Lord. This does not allow any room for doubt. In fact, the exact opposite

17

of Trust is Doubt. If you are fully Trusting in God, you cannot be exhibiting doubt in any fashion.

- Second, we are to LEAN NOT on our own understanding. Your own ideas, comprehension, perceptions, knowledge, and interpretation are simply that ... *your own*. If you depend on yourself, you leave no room for God to work!

One of the definitions of "hope" is to trust or to rely on something or someone. So, when we Trust in the Lord, we are HOPING in the Him-Possible! We have an expectation of fulfillment of that for which we pray.

In addition, when we STOP relying on ourselves and on our solutions, we PAUSE for the Him-Possible, as well! *We give God room to do what He does best!*

THE PAUSE

Today's scripture is so very familiar to most of us. But, I challenge you to look at it from a different perspective today. Speak your needs and requests in prayer. Then, say, "God I completely TRUST in You for the answers." Then, PAUSE with expectancy for God to perform the Him-Possible for you!

PRAYER & CONTEMPLATION:

God, there are so many things I do not understand in this life: Times of uncertainty and circumstances that cause me to question the outcome. But, I know that when I put my trust in You, and do not lean on my own understanding, You WILL direct my path, and it will become clearer with time. So, today, I will do my utmost to trust You to supply the best outcome for me and not to allow doubt to cloud my belief. In Jesus' name, Amen.

DAY 4-- Pause to STOP Worrying!   ME WORRY?

The use of euphemistic speech has nearly deserted us in this tell-all, bare-all, no-holds-barred world in which we live. I am so saddened by the lack of tact and decorum in our behaviors and conversations.

We think nothing of talking about "unmentionables" in public and in 'mixed company' (males and females in the same conversational circle). We use terms that would have made our grandmothers blush.

We don't bother to preserve someone's sensitive stomach when we talk graphically about losing the contents of ours (think regurgitate).

And yet, in spite of all our bold speech, we hesitate to call something what it really is. DOUBT is doubt. But, WORRY is also doubt. There are so many overlapping synonyms in the definitions of both these words: uncertainty, uneasiness, and apprehension, to name a few.

- Doubt= a feeling of uncertainty or lack of conviction.
- Worry= a state of anxiety and uncertainty.

We are more likely to say, "I feel uneasy" about something, rather than to declare our doubt. We feel more comfortable saying, "I'm apprehensive" about a situation, rather than to admit we are worried.

James lays it on the line in today's scripture:

- But let him ask in faith, with no doubting, for he who doubts is like a
  wave of the sea driven and tossed by the wind. ~James 1:6 *(NKJV)*

James declares that if you ask IN FAITH, you CANNOT have doubt — or worry, or apprehension, or uncertainty, or uneasiness — and expect to have a Him-Possible answer to your request!!!

He further explains, in no uncertain terms, what it means if you doubt when you pray (ask). You are like "a wave of the sea, driven and tossed by the wind." Can you catch a wave? Can you capture it and use it for a purpose? NO! Of course you can't!

That's because it moves all around, at the whim of the wind that drives it. Your doubt causes you to be unstable and is controlled by situations you see with your earthly, carnal vision, instead of by eyes of faith. Your "faith" is variable, instead of being steadfast, as God requires.

THE PAUSE

In exercising our faith today, I'm asking you to pray a BIG prayer of faith. Ask God for what you need Him to do. The more impossible it looks to be, the more faith you'll be required to exhibit. Say, "God, I can't, but you CERTAINLY can! I don't have to figure this out, because I completely, totally release it to You. Right now, I believe not only that You CAN, but that You WILL do the Him-Possible in my situation!!"

Don't worry, stress, waver, be apprehensive, uneasy, or indecisive about that statement of faith to God — Do. Not. Doubt. Do. Not. Worry.

Now, PAUSE   and wait for the Him-Possible to happen!

22

DAY 5-- Pause to Have Faith

In the children's book, "The Little Engine that Could," the small train is chugging uphill, chanting the entire way, "I think I can, I think I can." Eventually, when it reached the top, the train said, "I KNEW I could!"

The premise is, of course, that with faith and confidence in your abilities, you can do things that seem impossible to tackle.

When the man whose son was possessed by a spirit came to Jesus, he stated, "If You can do anything, have compassion on us and help us." The man had SOME faith, or he would never have come to Jesus with his need.

In today's verse, Jesus gives a strange response to the man:

- "If You can?" echoed Jesus. All things are possible to him who believes!
  ~Mark 9:23 *(Berean Study Bible)*

23

In other words, Jesus infers, "I'm ready to do the Him-Possible, but YOU must have the faith. YOU must believe! YOU must NOT doubt!!!"

Believing is having faith. Faith is confidence in God's abilities to perform the Him-Possible! We bring our need to Him, and then PAUSE.

Our pause is not a time to doubt. *It's a time to strengthen the faith we already had.* It's going from, "I think He can, I think He can," to "I KNEW He could!!!"

THE PAUSE

Does your need seem too big to get "over the mountain?" Does your 'engine' seem too small for the task? Then, stop trying to carry the load without faith! Say, "I KNOW He can! I KNOW He will!" Then, PAUSE to BELIEVE before you climb that last stretch over the mountain of Impossibility and view the Him-Possible from the top!

DAY 6 -- Pause to Confess

"Open confession is good for the soul."

~from Psalm 119:26

"Confessed faults are half-mended." *~Scottish proverb*

"A confession has to be part of your new life."

~Ludwig Wittgenstein

Confession is — acknowledgment; avowal; admission. A declaration or statement of belief.

We sometimes mistakenly believe a confession is the revealing of secret sins. That is one meaning, but confession is also declaring what you know to be true, while acknowledging a lack.

Continuing on with the account from yesterday's devotion, the man made a declaration or statement of belief. He followed this with a confession of his unbelief. *He acknowledged there was a lack, and he asked Jesus to HELP him believe.*

- Immediately the father of the child cried out and said with tears, "Lord, I believe; help my unbelief!" ~Mark 9:24 *(NKJV)*

Don't you just love how vulnerable and open the man becomes?! Jesus is able to operate fully at this point, because of the man's transparency. *He is now free to do the Him-Possible, because the man has PAUSED to confess!*

THE PAUSE

What part of your lack do you need to confess today? What confession will you "cry out with tears" to God, so that He can be free to do the Him-Possible?

God knows every part of your heart, so nothing is hidden from Him. God can work miracles with or without our participation. But, He loves to bestow miracles on those who Pause to Confess. We yield entirely our will to His in those moments.

And, an open, yielded heart is the perfect launching point for the Him-Possible to take place!

PRAYER & CONTEMPLATION:

God, as I look over my life today, I realize that there may be things I have not fully yielded to You. If there are parts of my mind, or my spirit, or my will that I am holding onto, thinking that I know best, then I turn that over to You today. I may have plans that I want to see fulfilled, but if those plans are preventing Your perfect will to be performed in me, then I hand them to You. I DO believe, God, but I confess that there may be remnants of unbelief in me, too. I am, after all, human. You know those parts of me better than anyone, so "help my unbelief," too! In Jesus' name, Amen.

DAY 7-- Pause to Look Up!

One of my favorite worship songs currently is "Looking Up," as sung by Nashville Life, and featuring vocalist CeCe Winans. The chorus alone is worth the listen, but there are two lines that thrill my soul with HOPE:

All of my problems are below You.
All that I need is in the palm of Your hands.

Did you catch that?! The problems aren't below US — they're below GOD!!! OUR problems are below HIM. Under our God's feet. We only need to focus upward. Not outward. Not inward. Certainly not downward. UPWARD. Look UP!

Secondly, every single thing that we could need is ready and waiting for us in the outstretched palm of God's hand! Instead of fretting, worrying, doubting, questioning, and "singing the blues" over what you lack— LOOK UP! He has it ready for you to choose from His hand.

28

When we look up, we don't see the never-ending swarm of problems that seemingly compass us. Our gaze focuses on Almighty God, and we see Him as the Conqueror. He is the Lord of Hosts. He commands the host of Heaven, and they march into battle FOR us.

Verse two references some encouraging concepts in the song—
- I won't be able to lose a battle, because it doesn't belong to me, but to God.
- Every single time I call on the name of Jesus, victory is imminent!

"EVERY TIME I call that name, I KNOW the victory is mine!" I don't doubt. I don't question. I don't waver. I KNOW my help comes from God!

- My help comes from the LORD, the Maker of heaven and earth. ~Psalm 121:2 *(NKJV)*

If God made the earth (and He did!), then don't you believe He is in control of it still? Don't you want the peace that comes from trusting in that Creator?

The bridge of "Looking Up" is so powerful, as it serves as a 'call and response' refrain! The question is asked of the listener: 'Where does my help come from?' The confident response is clear: 'It's coming from the Lord!' Consider the question in the following scripture—

- I lift up my eyes to the hills. From where does my help come?

~Psalm 121:1 *(ESV)*

The answer should *always* be your confident refrain: Your help, your healing, your salvation, your peace, your joy, your provision, your comfort -- ALL of it comes from the Lord!

THE PAUSE

We aren't oblivious to what's around us. But, we know that WE can't change any of it. *Instead, we choose to change the direction of our gaze.* We will look UP! What is the most important thing you can do today to see the Him-Possible happen in your life? *Change your focus from what you see around you, to the One who sees it all & who can do something about it.* All we need (the help we seek) comes from God! So, PAUSE and Look UP!!

PRAYER & CONTEMPLATION:

God, there is beauty all around us that we sometimes fail to see because we are too easily distracted by our limited eyesight. Lord, let me be like the child who lays in the grass and examines the sky for identifiable objects: a dog, an elephant, a horse. I want to look UP and see YOU! I want to identify You when I move my eyes from the mundane and murky situations in which I find myself. I desire to SEE the God of the Him-Possible when I lift my eyes—because You are where my help comes from! Help me remember to have child-like faith and to look UP. In Jesus' name, Amen.

DAY 8 -- Pause to Read the Signs!

One of the nastiest tasks that I volunteered to undertake at the church we pastored was to bring the aluminum cans home for recycling. You might ask how that could be nasty. All that's necessary is to toss them in a recycling bin somewhere, right?

♦♦ *Well, that would work, IF . . .*
Everyone would read and heed the signs! ♦♦

We had two trash cans in that specific area. One was clearly labeled, "ALUMINUM CANS ONLY." However, what I brought home was a conglomeration of icky trash amidst the cans!

Partly because I'm a little particular (okay, a LOT particular) about some things, the task required more than just recycling. To keep the bees away from the recycling bin, I would rinse all the sweet stickiness from the inside and outside of each can. A wiser, older person once informed me that crushing the cans gives you more "bang for your buck!" So, I used the crusher on them. And, the tabs were torn off & saved to donate to Ronald McDonald House Charities.

In other words, this voluntary task became quite a chore!

The worst part was the host of unidentifiable things that shared the sack with the cans! Sweetener packets, sucker sticks, 'used' gum, and coffee grounds are but a few of those things.

♦ *All because not everyone will read and heed the signs.* ♦

Even though the signs are clearly marked, they're missed by some. So, their oversight affects others.

When we fail to read and heed the signs that are clearly marked for us, we may cause others undue hardship. We may make their journey a little more difficult because of our neglect.

- For the time will come when they will not endure sound doctrine, but according to their own desires, because they have itching ears, they will heap up for themselves teachers; and they will turn their ears away from the truth, and be turned aside to fables. But you be watchful in all things, endure afflictions, do the work of an evangelist, fulfill your ministry.

~2 Timothy 4:3-5 *(NKJV)*

God has clearly "posted" the signs. It is up to us to read and heed them. Others may be distracted, or desirous of their own pleasure, and willingly reject what the signs tell them. But, our job is to be watchful (read the signs) and to fulfill our ministry (heed the signs).

THE PAUSE

Take time to read the signs that God has clearly marked for you. PAUSE. He wants you to pay attention to specific instructions He has given. Heed the signs that point to His return. Don't be distracted and toss trash in the same place that something redeemable is located.

The Him-Possible are those precious, redeemable souls who need to hear Truth and be cleaned & converted. *Our responsibility is to PAUSE & read the signs.* God's obligation, then, is to redeem the Him-Possible!

PRAYER & CONTEMPLATION:

Lord, there are times You place clear signs in front of us, directing us to answers we seek. We ask today that You remove the blinders that cause us to focus on the wrong things, and to broaden our vision to include the signs that give direction. Our desire is to see the signs, read the signs, and most of all to heed the signs You place before us. In Jesus' name, Amen.

DAY 9-- Pause to Be Strengthened

Building (carpentry work), painting walls & ceilings, laying concrete, mowing lawns, hoeing the garden, roofing a house, and many other manual labor jobs tax the body and deplete the strength of a person. Making time for respite is not a slothful act, but is necessary to replenish one's energy.

Any kind of hard physical labor requires times of rest. It may not be for a long period, but your body necessitates moments to reset; to regain its strength before continuing. You need a PAUSE to strengthen.

When it comes to Faith — and not doubting — one of the best Biblical examples is that of Abraham. In order to obey God, he had to:

- leave his current home for parts unknown
- be willing to operate out of his comfort zone
- live a nomadic life and cart his belongings with him everywhere

- travel through hostile and uncertain territory
- practice negotiation techniques on both humans and angelic (theophanic) creatures

Whew. I'm thinking we should take some lessons from the man with all that experience!

The point is, no matter how much faith Abraham displayed, he had to Pause at various times to be strengthened in his faith.

> - He did not waver at the promise of God through unbelief, but was strengthened in faith, giving glory to God.
> ~Romans 4:20 *(NKJV)*

He didn't waver—he didn't doubt or disbelieve—but stood strong. It was hard work to keep believing in a promise made so long before. He most likely might have been exhausted at the long, arduous journey he had undertaken.

But once he PAUSED to strengthen his Faith, he could give glory to God! The promise WAS coming. His consistent efforts WOULD pay off! And, although Abraham would be doing a lot of the "legwork," ultimately GOD would receive the glory for fulfilling the Him-Possible!!!

THE PAUSE

Are you laboring hard, and in need of respite? Do you feel you're wandering into parts unknown, and need to reset your GPS? Is the promise you received so far removed that you wonder if it's still on the horizon?

Then, it's time for you to PAUSE. Be strengthened in your faith—in Jesus' powerful, restorative name! Take some time to *make a physical list* of all the things you know that God has done for you in the past. You could even add some testimonies of others, as well -- faith-building reports that solidify your confidence in God's abilities to answer.

Do not waver. Do not doubt. Believe for your promise(s). Simply reading the list of what God HAS done will strengthen you to believe for what He WILL do. God IS going to do the Him-Possible—and you will gladly give Him the glory He deserves.

DAY 10-- Pause to Pray Everywhere

When they feel a song in their hearts, little children will break forth in singing. They do not care where they are, nor who is around. They are likely to be loud, possibly off-tune, and probably will rearrange (or make up) words, if they don't know them.

Bottom line: they're unashamed. What's inside MUST come out. Bystanders and spectators are welcome to observe or even join in. But, the children WILL sing, regardless.

In his first letter to Timothy, the Apostle Paul gave instructions and encouragement to the church to pray EVERY WHERE. In effect, Paul is saying, *"Pause in your everyday life—to pray. Pause while you're at work—to pray. Pause while you're in the marketplace—to pray. Pause when you're home—to pray. Pause when you are traveling—to pray."*

- I will therefore that men pray every where, lifting up holy hands, without wrath and doubting. ~1 Timothy 2:8 *(KJV)*

In other words, when you feel the prayers inside of you bubbling over, Pause—to pray. With a repentant heart, make certain you can lift holy hands to pray. Dedicated, consecrated, hallowed hands. Hands that don't and haven't partaken of sinful habits and activities. Hands that are clean.

Paul adds these words in the last part of the scripture: "without wrath and doubting." What does that have to do with praying everywhere?

Some versions say, *"without anger or dissension."* If you're angry, can you pray effectively? If you're in the middle of an argument, do you feel like blessing and praising God? If you strongly disagree with your friends or co-workers, and you've voiced your opinion in no uncertain terms, is it easy to raise your hands and pray at that moment?

The answer is, "NO!" Unequivocally no.

In addition, the anger inhibits or even prevents Faith from working through your prayers. So, Doubt is present, causes you to waver, and Faith is diminished.

NO prayer is unheard by God. But, faithless or doubting prayers tell God you don't believe what you're saying!

The reason children are uninhibited in vocalizing their songs is because they believe they CAN sing. They believe their song NEEDS to be heard. NO DOUBT is allowed.

THE PAUSE

At first, this PAUSE requires a lot of conscious thought or intentionality. Setting aside a place and a time to pray may warrant serious consideration of your circumstances. You might not be comfortable praying in various locations. In fact, it may be difficult to find a place or a time to pray throughout your day. But, making this kind of prayer a habit and a natural part of your spiritual lifestyle will soon become vital, if you want to see miraculous things occur!

41

When you Pause to pray — everywhere — BELIEVE what you're praying needs to be heard ... by God and sometimes by others. God wants to see and hear you pray Faith-filled prayers. Others will be affected by them, too. You'll be able to watch God perform the Him-Possible in your family's, friends' and co-workers' lives!

PRAYER & CONTEMPLATION:

Lord, today I ask for boldness. Please don't let my personality quirks keep me from praying when and where I need to do so. I may have used shyness as my excuse in the past. Or, the attributes of forwardness I may possess might at times be a hindrance to others listening to my witness. I ask that You show me how to be "wise as a serpent, yet harmless as a dove." Then, I can pray everywhere, and I know those prayers will be effective. In Jesus' name, Amen.

DAY 11 -- Pause to Please God

People-pleasers. Do you know any? Are *you* one? These are those who go to extremes to make others happy. Their solitary goal appears to be others' happiness.

For the most part, we recognize this as a particular character trait of some people. However, it is impossible to please 100% of the people 100% of the time. So, people-pleasers often suffer much angst because of this.

However, there IS Someone whom we should ALL strive to please. Fortunately for us, He has given us clear guidelines for ways we CAN please Him. And ways we do NOT.

If you really want to please God, you MUST have Faith. Do. Not. Doubt. God is so insistent on this prerequisite that He declares it is IMPOSSIBLE to please Him without it!!

- But without faith it is impossible to please Him, for he who comes to God must believe that He is, and that He is a rewarder of those who diligently seek Him.

  ~Hebrews 11:6 *(NKJV)*

With people-pleasers, the reward for their efforts is to see others happy & smiling. They typically don't seek more reward or recognition than this. Making you happy makes them happy; it's as simple as that.

In pleasing God, though, He promises rewards to those who BELIEVE (have Faith), and who DILIGENTLY seek Him. I suppose we aren't privy to exactly *what* the rewards will be, but we can be assured that we will be happy with them! In other words, we--as God-pleasers--will get more than the reward of making Him happy. *He has more in store for us that will add to our happiness.*

THE PAUSE

The caveat, though, is this: we are <u>required</u> to Pause to Please Him. It's another of those intentional tasks: *actively*

demonstrating our belief in Him and His abilities, and
conscientiously pursuing God.

Ask yourself these questions: How *can* I actively
demonstrate my faith? How *am* I actively demonstrating
my faith? And then, honestly assess your level of diligence.
Am I carefully and meticulously searching for God's
direction in my life on a daily basis? Once we PAUSE to
please Him by our Faith, He rewards us in return! Our
diligence also pays off. He does the Him-Possible for us.
What a win-win deal!

PRAYER & CONTEMPLATION:

God, in my pause today, let me use this time to reflect on
ways I can show my faith. I don't want my faith to be
demonstrated so only others can see it, as if I'm trying to
please them and garner a favorable opinion. Instead, let
my faith be bold, undaunted by circumstances, and
sincere. Because, <u>that's</u> the kind of faith You're looking for,
and it's You I desire to please. In Jesus' name, Amen.

DAY 12-- Pause to Hear

You may have seen those memes or heard the jokes about turning the car radio down so you can SEE better? It turns out there's actually a scientific explanation why this is so. But to make it simple to understand, it has to do with concentration and divided attention.

Our brain has to process important information correctly in order to effectively perform complex multitasking activities like driving. External distractions, like the radio, keep us from doing so.

My dad used to ask me if I heard him when he spoke. I'd reply, "Yes, Dad, I heard you." Because he could easily tell I was distracted, his response was, "You heard me, but you weren't listening."

Oh, that frustrated me! Only because it was the truth — and I had been caught! I heard his words being spoken,

but distractions kept me from processing their meaning.
And, he could clearly detect that lack of focused attention.

If only I had PAUSED, really listened, and processed the
meaning, my actions would reflect that I had HEARD.

- So then faith comes by hearing, and hearing
  by the word of God. ~Romans 10:17 *(NKJV)*

If you want to access Faith — believing, trusting, having
confidence in someone or something — you have to 'turn
the radio down.' *The outside noises and influences may be
what is keeping you from seeing clearly.* Get rid of the
distractions and truly HEAR the Word of God! Then watch
your FAITH increase!

THE PAUSE

PAUSE to hear the Word—when you read it, when it's
spoken, when it's preached. Undistracted hearing will be
reflected in our ACTIONS. We will demonstrate what we
have heard and believe.

- Thus also faith by itself, if it does not have works, is dead. But someone will say, "You have faith, and I have works." Show me your faith without your works, and I will show you my faith by my works.

  ~James 2:17-18 *(NKJV)*

We can add works to our faith and our actions will showcase our Faith. We will speak words into the atmosphere that prove to God that we BELIEVE His Word. When we operate in another realm by displaying our action-backed faith, God cannot help but honor that.

That great Faith, then, releases God to do the Him-Possible!!!

DAY 13 -- Pause to Walk

Remembering the games of my childhood, I fondly recall playing Blind Man's Bluff (tag), Pin the Tail on the Donkey, and Taste Test. The commonality of these games is that they require a blindfold to play.

Although being blindfolded removes the sense of sight while playing, all your other senses become heightened and grow keener to compensate. In addition, you must TRUST in order to play successfully.

- Blind Man's Bluff - you have to LISTEN to every sound, learning to distinguish movement and direction. You'll need to TOUCH objects & people, in your sightless search for someone to tag.

- Pin the Tail on the Donkey - you have to TOUCH objects in your path, allowing you to locate the desired target. Sometimes others will try to "guide" you to the object. This requires TRUST in your helpers' abilities to steer you correctly.

- Taste Test - your sense of SMELL must come to the forefront when identifying a food choice which you cannot see. Depending on the game's rules where you're playing, you may be able to TOUCH the food, to feel its texture and help in identification.

As with these games, our lives can seem like we're trying to maneuver blindfolded! We often have to determine what is the most effective way to deal with situations when we cannot SEE which way to turn.

Walking with God is an exercise in TRUST. He will not steer you wrong, or try to persuade you to get off track. But, we can only move forward when we Do. Not. Doubt.

- For we walk by faith, not by sight.
  ~2 Corinthians 5:7 (NKJV)

Believe. Trust. Be Convinced. Be Confident in. You have to allow your other spiritual senses to grow keener. Make provision for heightened spiritual awareness as you walk forward in Christ.

THE PAUSE

Most of all, just PAUSE. *Get your spiritual bearings.* Don't try to SEE with natural eyes what is only meant for spiritual eyes of discernment. You may have to FEEL out your surroundings. Determine if WHAT is around you fits what you know should be a part of your life. Determine if WHO is around you is capable of giving you sure guidance to your destination.

- Beloved, do not believe every spirit, but test the spirits, whether they are of God; because many false prophets have gone out into the world. ~1 John 4:1 *(NKJV)*

Pause ... and then WALK. *Take the next step.* Trusting. Believing. IN Faith! WITH Faith. THROUGH Faith. Then, as you walk in Faith, the HIM-POSSIBLE will come to pass — right before both your natural AND your spiritual eyes!

DAY 14-- Pause for Inspiration

Have you ever participated in a group project that went awry? Even though the planning went well, the brainstorming was quick and productive, and everything looked good on paper—somehow it flopped.

You may have heard someone sarcastically say, "Whose bright idea was this anyway?" Suddenly, it seemed like a bad scheme.

But, the whole concept of a "bright idea" is actually a positive one. It is defined as "a clever thought or new idea" *(McGraw-Hill Dictionary of American Idioms and Phrasal Verbs)* and as "a unique or shrewd thought." *(Farlex Dictionary of Idioms)*

So, where is the *best* place to "get" a bright idea, then? How about from a place of brightness—from the Light?!

Inspiration literally means,

1. the act of drawing in, specifically: the drawing of air into the lungs.

2. a divine influence or action on a person believed to qualify him or her to receive and communicate sacred revelation. *(Merriam-Webster)*

I've often heard it defined as "God-breathed," so when you feel inspired with a unique or clever thought, thank God for filling your lungs with air and your mind with great ideas!

God not only *gives* inspiration, He enjoys demonstrating inspiration! He declares that doing something new, something unique, something unusual is something of which to take note.

- Behold, I will do a new thing, Now it shall spring forth; Shall you not know it? I will even make a road in the wilderness *And* rivers in the desert.

    ~Isaiah 43:19 *(NKJV)*

Bright ideas. A Brainstorm. An Illuminating Realization. Enlightenment.

- But if we walk in the light as He is in the light, we have fellowship with one another, and the blood of Jesus Christ His Son cleanses us from all sin.
~1 John 1:7 *(NKJV)*

We WALK in the Light. We are illuminated by His brightness. *He provides benefits, such as great fellowship and a soul-cleansing.*

- Do not rejoice over me, my enemy; When I fall, I will arise; When I sit in darkness, The LORD will be a light to me.
~Micah 7:8 *(NKJV)*

When everything looks bleak, you can rest assured the Light is not far away. The enemy tries to tell you your bright ideas were duds. His lies try to convince you that no one cares about your clever thoughts and unique ideas; that God can't use you OR your "bright ideas." Lies, lies, lies.

THE PAUSE

While walking through this day, PAUSE & open yourself up to all the possibilities that God provides to inspire you. If you feel you've received some really great ideas of ministry opportunities or creative openings, do not hesitate to write these ideas down somewhere. Keep a list of them. Pray about them. Ask God to further enlighten you about ways you can incorporate them in your life to better further the Kingdom. He has some "bright ideas" for you and some Him-Possible ways to use them!

PRAYER & CONTEMPLATION:

Dear Lord, YOU are the source of inspiration that I desire to obtain. Throughout this day, let me be aware of the details that indicate Your presence. In the simple things I see, may I realize there is a lesson there for me, if I look and listen to Your voice. In my interaction with others, give me fresh sparks of wisdom and understanding, so that my relationships will flourish. In Jesus' name, Amen.

DAY 15--Pause to be Encouraged!

"Keep it up!" "Atta-boy!" "Good job!" "You're doing great!"

Did you smile, reading those encouraging phrases? Hearing (reading) words of encouragement brings about smiles, grins, and lifted shoulders. Yes, when someone speaks those positive words to you, something changes in the atmosphere around you.

Encouragement is a vital part of a person's continuous walk with God. Sometimes we hear encouragement from others. Sometimes we have to give ourselves a pep talk. Yes, talking to yourself is acceptable--especially if you're doing it to bring encouragement to yourself during a time of despondency. King David found it necessary, but showed us the key to being successful with your motivational speech: Encourage yourself IN THE LORD.

- And David was greatly distressed; for the people spake of stoning him, because the soul of all the people was grieved, every man for his sons and for his daughters: but David encouraged himself in the LORD his God. ~1 Samuel 30:6 *(KJV)*

Maybe you are feeling dejected, or weary. Maybe you don't think you can complete the task, and your confidence level is at an all-time low. Maybe you feel like a failure. Maybe your "win" column appears much smaller than your "lose" column.

You aren't alone. The spectators are waiting to cheer you on to victory! Their "Atta-boys!" and " Keep it Ups!" give you much-needed strength and an emotional lift. You gain enough from the words of encouragement to finish what you started.

KEEP IT UP! Be encouraged. Stay encouraged. Be an encourager. Do not be afraid of building others up. It won't make you look smaller or less important. Contrariwise, it will make you a much bigger and better person for taking the time to bless someone else. A bonus to encouraging others: you also bring encouragement to yourself.

- Therefore encourage one another and build each other up, just as in fact you are doing.
  ~1 Thessalonians 5:11 *(NIV)*

THE PAUSE

This is not the time to give up. It's the time to PAUSE to be encouraged -- and to encourage others. Yes, this is also the time to PAUSE to spur one another ON. "Keep it up!" Don't give in. Don't falter. *You never know how close someone may be to giving up, to not showing up, to secluding themselves away from the Body of Christ.* Your encouragement can make all the difference!

- And let us consider how we may spur one another on toward love and good deeds, not giving up meeting together, as some are in the habit of doing, but encouraging one another—and all the more as you see the Day approaching. ~Hebrews 10:24-25 (*NIV*)

God has some mighty HIM-POSSIBLE things He wants to do through you. For you. With you. To you. The key to seeing those mighty things? KEEP IT UP!

PRAYER & CONTEMPLATION:

God, there are days and times when I feel my own strength flagging. No doubt, it even appears to others that I am faltering in my faith and determination. It is in those times, that I need Your "atta-boys" more than any others. In the same way, may You make me aware of others who need encouragement, and give me the words that will help them through their own struggles. If I only seek help for myself, I have failed to be the hands and feet that You've called me to be for those around me. So for today, give ME strength, but also let me BE strength and support for others. In Jesus' name, Amen.

DAY 16-- Pause to Be Silent

For the next few days, we will be focusing on a group of people who struggled to believe; who doubted. From these, I hope to use the 'negative' aspects to point us to greater faith!

ZECHARIAH, the priest.

1. First recorded angelic visitation of the New Testament era was to him.
2. A good and righteous man.
3. Fulfilling his role as priest (doing what was right & minding his own business).
4. Consistent, faithful, & chosen by God to fulfill an amazing role in the big Kingdom picture.
5. Human. Astounded, taken by surprise, and expressed some valid concerns.

- 18 Zechariah asked the angel, "How can I be sure of this? I am an old man and my wife is well along in years."
- 19 The angel said to him, "I am Gabriel. I stand in the presence of God, and I have been sent to speak to you and to tell you this good news.
- 20 And now you will be silent and not able to speak until the day this happens, because you did not believe my words, which will come true at their appointed time."

~Luke 1:18-20 *(NIV)*

I honestly don't blame Zechariah. I would likely have responded the same. (And so would you have, probably!) He stated the obvious—they WERE both old. From my standpoint, his question seemed innocent enough: "How can I be sure of this?"

Apparently, in his case, that question was the wrong one to ask of an angel! Gabriel emphatically declared his position, his mission, and finally, his declaration of punishment.

Zechariah received an immediate penalty for DOUBTING. Whoa!

♦ His PAUSE was a mandated one. He didn't get a choice about it. He was forced to BE SILENT. ♦

Now, here are some important factors to consider:

1. He was indeed visited by an angel with an important announcement! It would impact not only HIS life, but also his wife's life—and the future of all mankind.
2. He was still a good and righteous man. He wasn't punished for being evil.
3. He was still a priest. * His position and ministry were not taken away.*
4. He remained consistent, faithful, and chosen by God. That is apparent in his response to those questioning the choice of the baby's name. Those traits were also carefully instilled in his promised son, as evidenced by John's ministry.
5. ♦♦ His humanity was the necessary means by which the miraculous could occur! Zechariah's obvious observations

became tools in the Hands of God for a truly Supernatural demonstration of the Him-Possible!!! ◆◆

THE PAUSE

Now, to bring this to where we live.

- Sometimes God has to mandate silence from us, in order for His will to be performed in us, unimpeded.
- When God wants us to keep silence, we aren't being punished because we are bad or sinful.
- We can continue in our current ministry while awaiting the Him-Possible.
- We MUST be consistent and faithful—regardless of how impossibly long the miracle is taking to arrive.

◆◆ If you want to see the HIM-POSSIBLE happen, just present your humanity as a tool for God to use.◆◆

DAY 17-- Pause to Cry Out

Today, we examine a second example of 'negative' faith:

THE DISCIPLES, on the boat.

1. They were Jesus' chosen followers. Hand-picked. Set apart for a purpose.
2. They were doing a good thing. Jesus needed a respite from the crowds.
3. They didn't ask for the storm.
4. Their prior experiences made them concerned. Their natural, human instinct was fear in that situation.
5. They were not faithless. Their trust was placed in their Master's abilities.

- 18 And when Jesus saw great multitudes about Him, He gave a command to depart to the other side.

- 23 Now when He got into a boat, His disciples followed Him.
- 24 And suddenly a great tempest arose on the sea, so that the boat was covered with the waves. But He was asleep.
- 25 Then His disciples came to Him and awoke Him, saying, "Lord, save us! We are perishing!"
- 26 But He said to them, "Why are you fearful, O you of little faith?" Then He arose and rebuked the winds and the sea, and there was a great calm.

~Matthew 8:18, 23-26 *(NKJV)*

Every time the disciples finally thought they "had it right," something else came along to test their faith. They watched miracle after miracle being performed by this man they so willingly followed. And, yet, when faced with common, everyday opportunities for them to grow their faith, they failed again.

This would really be tough for most of us. In fact, I can actually empathize with those guys. Seems I also fail the same tests repeatedly.

◆ *In the middle of the test, they PAUSED. Yes, they froze. Their instinctive reaction was to cry out. But, that response was an indication of their LACK of faith. They DOUBTED.*◆

Again, here are some important factors to consider:

1. They were receiving instruction on a daily basis on how to behave as Disciples. The Teacher invested His time in them, and He expected more of them than He did of the crowd.
2. Their good deed was performed for the Master's benefit. They obeyed immediately when called on to take Him to the other side of the lake. They may have thought that would exempt them from potential danger.
3. The storm came on suddenly. *It was an unexpected obstacle.* After the emotional highs of watching so many miracles, the last thing they wanted was disaster to befall them.

4. ♦ In spite of their recognition that Jesus WAS the Promised One, their humanity kicked in — and they felt real fear. They faltered in their faith. ♦

5. However, they were NOT without faith. They may have doubted their own abilities, but their faith remained constant in HIS abilities.

They PAUSED to cry out for His help. Although he reprimanded them for not having ENOUGH faith, He still performed the Him-Possible for them. He calmed the storm. Immediately.

THE PAUSE

OH, my! What a beautiful assurance this example of 'negative' faith actually provides us!!

- Although we cry out for God's help in the middle of the storm, He answers and calms it, DESPITE our lack of faith.
- We may think we know God because we've spent time with Him. But, His expectations of us are higher, BECAUSE of what He's taught us. *He looks*

for opportunities to watch us put into action what we have learned from Him.

- The unexpected obstacle is often frightening. While we see the storm and feel the danger, Jesus is resting. He's waiting on US to use the faith we DO have to believe for the miraculous!

♦♦ The Him-Possible WILL happen, though, when we
PAUSE to cry out
to the Master of every storm. He will not withhold His
power when we
ask for His help, despite our own insecurities. ♦♦

For we walk by faith, not by sight
II Corinthians 5:7

DAY 18-- Pause to See Jesus, and NOT the Wind

Our third example of 'negative' faith is none other than:

PETER, walking on the water.

1. Location. He was in that boat, on that lake, at that time because of obedience to Jesus.
2. Circumstances. He also didn't ask for the high waves and strong winds he & the others were experiencing.
3. Character. He was bold enough to speak to what they all supposed was a ghost.
4. Readiness. He was willing to take a huge step of faith — right off the side of the boat!
5. Weakness. His humanity and an awareness of the dangers caused him to lose focus.

- 26 And when the disciples saw Him walking on the sea, they were troubled, saying, "It is a ghost!" And they cried out for fear.
- 27 But immediately Jesus spoke to them, saying, "Be of good cheer! It is I; do not be afraid."
- 28 And Peter answered Him and said, "Lord, if it is You, command me to come to You on the water."
- 29 So He said, "Come." And when Peter had come down out of the boat, he walked on the water to go to Jesus.
- 30 But when he saw that the wind was boisterous, he was afraid; and beginning to sink he cried out, saying, "Lord, save me!"
- 31 And immediately Jesus stretched out His hand and caught him, and said to him, "O you of little faith, why did you doubt?" ~Matthew 14:26-31 *(NKJV)*

♦ Peter—impetuous, bold, daring, and a bit reckless. His personality was both a propellant and a hindrance to him. ♦

His brashness allowed him to take risks without caring what others thought. But, his impetuosity also caused him to second-guess the wisdom of his decisions.

Some factors to consider:

1. Jesus asked for time alone. He sent them ahead by boat. Peter obeyed without question or argument.
2. As an experienced fisherman, Peter knew there was always a possibility of bad weather on the lake. After a long day with Jesus—feeding multitudes and seeing miracles performed—he probably hoped for smooth sailing...NOT for the sudden weather change!
3. Peter's boldness on this night was a propellant to experiencing a miracle. The others with him were afraid and timid, and wouldn't even speak to Jesus.
4. So much has been said about Peter's failure that night. BUT, his FAITH is what caused him to take that initial step out of that boat.
5. The noise of wind and crashing waves were enough to distract Peter. ◆*Carnality interfered with a supernatural act of faith!*◆

Peter's one mistake was when he PAUSED. His Him-Possible miracle was already in motion.

♦ *It was his response to his surroundings that caused him to lose focus.* ♦

The REALLY interesting thing about this account is that every Bible version states that Peter SAW the wind. NOT that he heard the wind, or even that he saw the results of the wind.

Peter PAUSED and SAW the wind "boisterous." ♦*He interrupted his own miracle by looking at the wrong thing!!*♦

The wind was already buffeting the boat. Nothing new. The waves were already crashing around him. Nothing new. The night was already dark. Nothing new. Jesus came walking on the water toward the boat. DEFINITELY something new!

But, his DOUBT came when he SAW —focused— on something that was previously occurring even before his miracle began.

THE PAUSE

These things we can glean from Peter's 'negative' faith experience:

1. We can be in complete obedience to God's will and still face some strong winds and fierce waves.
2. Adversity doesn't mean disaster is impending. *It means we are preparing for the Him-Possible!*
3. God can give you boldness to step out with the little faith you DO possess.
4. The wind WILL buffet you. The waves WILL crash against you. The night WILL be dark.
5. <u>Just don't LOOK AT (SEE) the wind.</u>
♦*Don't focus on what's CAUSING havoc around you.*♦
PAUSE to SEE Jesus...and Keep Walking!

DAY 19-- Pause to Reach

Another character who illustrated 'negative' faith was nicknamed because of it—'Doubting Thomas.'

THOMAS, after the resurrection.

1. Thomas was a good guy, chosen by Jesus to be one of 'the twelve.' Not a lot was written about him in the gospels, so we could say, 'No news is good news' where he is concerned.

2. He happened to be in the wrong place at the wrong time when Jesus had appeared earlier to the others, shortly after His resurrection.

3. We can surmise that Thomas was a twin. His surname, Didymus, means "twin" or "double." Perhaps he was used to having to PROVE himself; to "be his own man."

4. Because of this trait, he may have required evidence, in order to completely see things as true. His statement, "EXCEPT I see...I will NOT believe" bears this out.

5. Thomas's very words were used by Jesus when it was time to prove the facts to him.

- 24 But Thomas, one of the twelve, called Didymus, was not with them when Jesus came.
- 25 The other disciples therefore said unto him, We have seen the Lord. But he said unto them, Except I shall see in his hands the print of the nails, and put my finger into the print of the nails, and thrust my hand into his side, I will not believe.
- 26 And after eight days again his disciples were within, and Thomas with them: then came Jesus, the doors being shut, and stood in the midst, and said, Peace be unto you.
- 27 Then saith he to Thomas, Reach hither thy finger, and behold my hands; and reach hither thy hand, and thrust it into my side: and be not faithless, but believing.

~John 20:24-27 *(KJV)*

◆ Thomas may have gotten a 'bad rap' over time because of his lack of trust. We know he DID express doubt. But he also let his faith grow when it was needed. ◆

'Doubting Thomas' didn't WANT to be negative. He just wanted PROOF. This whole concept of Jesus' resurrection would solidify and validate the Gospel message. That was too important to Thomas to depend on the words of others. He needed to see it for himself!

HOWEVER...the need for proof was evidence of Thomas's disbelief. He DOUBTED, when he should have trusted and had faith.

Factors to consider:

1. Thomas was NOT present when Jesus showed Himself to the others. He may have felt "out of the loop" because of this.
2. A full eight days passed between one visitation of Jesus to the next. That allowed more time for Thomas's doubt to grow.

3. Jesus emphasized over and over how important BELIEVING was, especially without SEEING.

4. Thomas PAUSED for "Except," and specified his restrictions. *This Pause took away a large portion of his faith.*

5. When Jesus visited again, He gave Thomas a new PAUSE. Thomas now had to Pause to REACH. Jesus expected him to work for his Faith!

One of the most important components of Thomas's conversion from Doubter to Believer was his face-to-face encounter with Jesus.

He was humbled by what he saw. Truth was evident in front of him. No false substitute could or would know SO much about Thomas.

♦ His humility opened the door for revelation to enter: "My Lord, and my God!" *(verse 28)* ♦

THE PAUSE

Some lessons we can glean from Thomas's 'negative' faith:

- We may not have the privilege of being present when the first Him-Possible answer comes!
- ♦ *When we add our own exceptions and restrictions to what we hope to see Jesus accomplish, we negate pure faith.* ♦
- Because Jesus is gracious, however, and mindful of our human weaknesses, He will often provide a second opportunity to witness the Him-Possible.
- ♦♦ When DOUBT comes face-to-face with TRUTH, we cannot help but be humbled. With our humility comes REVELATION! ♦♦
- Jesus will sometimes make us WORK to increase our Faith! He will ask us to PAUSE — to REACH. *Stretching ourselves to touch what we KNOW is Truth will make us believers in the Him-Possible!*

DAY 20-- Pause to Be Troubled

Today's focus on 'negative' faith is a group, rather than an individual.

THE ELEVEN, after the resurrection.

1. The disciples are still meeting together, even though Jesus — their leader — was taken from them.
2. At this point, Peter & John, as well as the ladies (Mary Magdalene, Joanna, Mary—the mother of James, and others) had witnessed the empty tomb.
3. Still, they did not believe.
4. There were two others, Simon & Cleopas, who had encountered Jesus on the road to Emmaus. They also ran back to the Eleven, to share the news.
5. They still did not believe. That's when Jesus appeared suddenly in their midst.

- 33 So they rose up that very hour and returned to Jerusalem, and found the eleven and those who were with them gathered together,
- 34 And saying, "The Lord is risen indeed, and has appeared to Simon!"
- 35 And they told about the things that had happened on the road, and how He was known to them in the breaking of bread.
- 36 Now as they said these things, Jesus Himself stood in the midst of them, and said to them, "Peace to you."
- 37 But they were terrified and frightened, and supposed they had seen a spirit.
- 38 And He said to them, "Why are you troubled? And why do doubts arise in your hearts? ~ Luke 24:33-38 *(NKJV)*

The book of Mark also recounts this occurrence:

- 14 Later He appeared to the eleven as they sat at the table; and He rebuked their unbelief and hardness of heart, because

they did not believe those who had seen
Him after He had risen.

~Mark 16:14 *(NKJV)*

Some factors to consider:

1. They were totally shaken by the events of the preceding days.
2. They had just seen their leader killed for the teachings to which they adhered. They were afraid for their lives also.
3. Although some of them had witnessed the empty tomb, it was still hard to comprehend in their human thinking that Jesus could possibly be alive.
4. The women's testimony of what the angel AND Jesus had said to them seemed foolishness to the Eleven. <u>They gave it little credence.</u>
5. Even when Jesus DID appear in their midst, they thought he was a ghost. It was sudden. It was unnatural. It was a bit frightening (as we all might feel, too).

The Eleven wanted so badly to believe. They had stuck with Jesus even when He was ridiculed. Jesus had even further explained parables to them, so they'd understand Kingdom principles.

They had just witnessed some very awful and traumatic events. They were quite on edge and trying to decide where to go and how to respond from here. *Their belief system had just been shaken at its core.*

So...given all these factors, when Jesus did appear, they were frightened—a very natural response. *They PAUSED to be troubled.*

But, Jesus immediately rebuked them for their fear AND their unbelief. He questioned them about both, digging deeply into their thoughts and feelings. Not only were there doubts in their minds, there were doubts in their hearts. The seat of their emotions was in turmoil.

THE PAUSE

Some great things we can learn from their experience:

- Events that seem traumatic and insurmountable can cause us to DOUBT.
- The Word doesn't lie, <u>but our humanity often conflicts with what we KNOW to be true about God.</u>
- Others can testify of what Him-Possible things God has done and revealed to them. But their testimonies may seem as 'nonsense' to us; hard to comprehend the magnitude of the Him-Possible!
- ♦ *Our troubled PAUSE can be the very moment we realize God is AWARE of our thoughts and feelings and is working to dispel our fears!* ♦
- Their 'negative' faith caused them unrest and confusion. Their PAUSE to be troubled did NOT stop the Him-Possible from happening!

♦ God STILL appears to confirm His presence in our lives, even when our human responses are not what He wishes they were. ♦

The Him-Possible will happen for us when we least expect it! Get ready, for it WILL happen!!

DAY 21-- Pause to Step It Up! (Re-Energize)

Have you ever been with someone who moved so slowly you almost wanted to walk FOR them?! Lagging behind is usually not a desirable outcome. Others move ahead, and the one unhurriedly strolling gets further and further behind.

Sometimes a coach will encourage a player to move a little faster. He/she knows the player has it in them to pick up speed without compromising their health or well-being.
♦ *They just need encouragement and motivation.* ♦

STEP IT UP! Move a little faster. Don't lag behind. Increase the pace. These are all phrases one might hear from a coach or from the supporters on the sidelines. *They should motivate the participant to press forward with even greater fervor than before.* These are not critical statements of one's inabilities. Rather, they are positive reinforcement from those who care to encourage one's progress!

- not lagging in diligence, fervent in spirit, serving the Lord; ~Romans 12:11 *(NKJV)*

I also love the way the Berean Study Bible interprets this passage:

- Do not let your zeal subside; keep your spiritual fervor, serving the Lord.
  ~Romans 12:11 *(BSB)*

Specifically, this passage is a continuation of the giftings a person receives from God — prophesying, serving, teaching, giving, encouraging, leading, and showing mercy. *(Romans 12:6-8)* These are followed closely by commands to love sincerely. *(Romans 12:9-10) And THEN, we are admonished to not lag in diligence.*

STEP IT UP! *The Pause you should take is one that re-energizes you to diligently and fervently fulfill your calling!*

Don't Pause *(lag)* to Doubt. Don't Pause *(lag)* to compare. Don't Pause *(lag)* to slow your forward progress. Don't Pause *(lag)* to quit.

THE PAUSE

I'm encouraging you today to STEP IT UP! *Pick up your pace & accomplish as much as you can for God and His Kingdom!* Move a little faster to win the lost, to share your testimony, to encourage, to give, to serve, to teach, to show mercy, and to love others.

STEP IT UP! ♦ The finish line is now in view. ♦ It's definitely not a time to give up and give in to fears. It IS a time to regroup and FINISH the race!

God truly wants to do the Him-Possible in your life. *All He needs is for you to STEP UP YOUR FAITH and to put it into action!*

DAY 22 -- Pause to Stir it Up! (Don't let it Settle)

You open a packet of Hot Chocolate mix, pour it in your cup, add boiling water, and stir. Not as good as homemade-from-scratch, but not bad either. Suddenly, you're called away for something. When you return, not only is the drink cold, the flavor is now weakened.

The contents of a variety of drinks and foods, when left unattended, can separate. To enjoy the best flavors, it's important to stir it up. Keep it viable. Make it workable.

God has given you a gift that is comprised of various layers: Faith, Prayer, Hope, and Joy, to name a few. With the passing of time, sometimes those components separate from one another. The gift is still there; it just doesn't work as well.

♦ *You must PAUSE and "reassemble" your gift.* ♦ It needs to be stirred up. Everything you need to make it viable is contained in it. It's up to you to bring all those separate good things together to make it the BEST gift.

If you distance yourself from Prayer, Joy settles to the bottom. If Faith is allowed to grow cold, Hope cannot be tasted. Doubt is what remains, *and doubt is not a workable component of God's gift to you — the Him-Possible.*

- Therefore I remind you to stir up the gift of God which is in you through the laying on of my hands. ~2 Timothy 1:6 *(NKJV)*

In this passage, Paul is reminding Timothy that he has genuine faith in him that was passed down from his mother & grandmother *(verse 5)*. But, he also encourages Timothy to STIR IT UP — to not let it settle.

THE PAUSE

I also encourage YOU today. Don't let your gift of Faith settle either. That beautiful gift needs a stirring of Prayer and Joy as you worship God. Pray specific prayers. Speak the Word over your requests: "God, You said that if we believe, anything is possible. I believe that I have received the thing I have prayed for; therefore, it will be mine." Then Hope will be mixed in, and finally, Faith WILL BE what it was intended to be.

- Now faith is the substance of things hoped for, the evidence of things not seen.

~Hebrews 11:1 *(KJV)*

Something with substance is visible. When our Hope becomes visible, via our actions that mirror our Faith, the evidence points to the fact that our Faith has been stirred up. It has become part of something even more exciting than when it stands alone.

It will be a potent and viable mixture that allows the Him-Possible to be done in your life!!

Be blessed ... and STIR IT UP!

DAY 23-- Pause to Be Tested

There is one particular area on a route that I used to travel regularly that is breathtaking on certain mornings. As the fog is lifting from the river valley, the cattle are grazing in the fields covered in dew. The bluffs above the river are barely visible, with wisps of fog covering them. And the river itself looks serene, as though waking peacefully from its foggy covering.

BUT...that same pastoral setting is an entirely different view as you enter the valley at night. When the fog settles over it all, visibility is severely limited. It's dark, and appears eerily quiet. Nocturnal creatures can quickly surprise you by darting onto the roadway. The car's headlights barely penetrate the heavy mist.

At those times, I have to trust my memory of the turns of the road. I have to rely on the light available to help navigate through the dangers of the fog. ♦ *The scariest part? I don't KNOW what's ahead.* ♦ My faith is tested, because at that point, I must simply believe.

> • knowing that the testing of your faith
>   produces patience.
>
> ~James 1:3 *(NKJV)*

Driving quickly would not help me navigate better. *Getting angry at the fog would not change its presence.* To curse the darkness will not cause the sun to rise prematurely. I must be patient to make it through safely. Driving through the night fog causes me to slow down. It's a test of my driving skills, to be sure. But, impatience will cause me to fail. Miserably.

No! Instead, I must PAUSE in my hurried journey to "take this test." It's part of measuring my success as a mature driver.

How well can I navigate through dense fog and darkness? Am I willing to slow down *(pause)* to trust the process of maneuvering through factors that impair my distant vision?

THE PAUSE

Many of us are indeed in a fog-covered valley at present. Darkness has descended for the time being. We can't control the fog, nor make it go away by hurrying through it. We can't force the sun to rise, to make the fog dissipate, or to lessen the dangers around us.

Instead, we must PAUSE to allow God to prove (test) our spiritual maturity. What 'skills' have we learned in our walk with God that will help us navigate safely? What is this testing teaching us as we move forward in experience?

◆◆ *The same fog that causes distress at night will bring a peaceful, serene sense of Faith as the sun rises.* ◆◆ The TEST of our Faith produces PATIENCE. {Other versions refer to it as "endurance," "perseverance," and "steadfastness."}

My Trust (Faith) in the process of successful navigation produces patience (perseverance) to bring me safely through the fog. It SEEMS impossible to make it through. But, my Faith will make it Him-Possible!!

DAY 24-- Pause to Rely on God's Strength

God is the Source
of our Strength

One of the hardest parts of watching people age is observing a loss of strength in their bodies. Most have been independent all their lives. It puts a dent in their pride to accept help in areas where they are no longer strong enough to cope.

- Lending a hand to help them negotiate difficult terrain.
- Placing an arm around them when they falter.
- Putting a palm under their elbow to walk alongside and steady them.

♦ These are all examples of folks relying on others and of others lending their strength to them. ♦

But, many times they look at these "helps" as threats to their independence. *Instead, it would be better if they thought of it as doubling their own strength.*

God gives us strong assurance in today's scripture that He will be alongside us to STRENGTHEN us when we are weak; to UPHOLD us when we falter. When we RELY on God's strength in our times of weakness, we will find our strength has doubled.

> • Fear not, for I am with you; Be not dismayed, for I am your God. I will strengthen you, Yes, I will help you, I will uphold you with My righteous right hand.'
> ~Isaiah 41:10 *(NKJV)*

THE PAUSE

When we are fearful *(anxious, uneasy, hesitant)* or dismayed *(disturbed, upset, uneasy)*, it's best to PAUSE and to rely on God's strength. Carrying on without consulting the One who can help us best is akin to trying to walk on a broken foot without the aid of a crutch or walking boot. We need some help. *The aid--whether material or human--is for our benefit, NOT to make us look or feel weak.*

'Fearful' and 'dismayed' both indicate a level of faithlessness or DOUBT. Instead of writing us off as unable to do what we must, God graciously comes alongside to HELP; to STRENGTHEN.

◆◆There is something so relieving when we realize that relying on God's strength is not making ourselves look weaker, but is granting us more strength than we would have on our own.◆◆

◆ He doubles our own strength.◆

He lends His support, so that we can be ready for the Him-Possible!!!

DAY 25-- Pause to Be Commanded

"Sit straight." "Stand up tall." "Look alive!" "Move it!" "Forward, March!"

Commands generally serve the purpose of gaining someone's attention AND of an answering response ... usually through action. Some synonyms for a command are 'an imperative' or 'an order.'

When a commander barks an order at a soldier, he/she expects obedience and for the order to be followed exactly. Sloppy responses or defiant opposition is NOT tolerated.

Yesterday's scripture was similar to today's, with one major difference: today's scripture reminds us of God's specific COMMANDS.

- Have I not commanded you? Be strong and of good courage; do not be afraid, nor be dismayed, for the LORD your God is with you wherever you go." ~Joshua 1:9 *(NKJV)*

God commanded Joshua and the people of Israel to BE STRONG, to BE OF GOOD COURAGE, to NOT BE AFRAID, NOR to be DISMAYED. Commands—not suggestions. Orders—not proposals.

♦ Courage requires a Lack of Doubt.♦ Being strong demands that no weakness be displayed. No Doubt can be shown. Exhibiting confidence in your own abilities to tackle a difficult situation, yes. *But, more importantly, having confidence in GOD'S ability to accomplish the Him-Possible!*

An extremely comforting part of God's command is His reassurance to us: He will be right with us WHEREVER WE GO. *God not only provides the help we need, He also never leaves our side.* It's a promise.

THE PAUSE

So, as you walk through this present battle of uncertainty, PAUSE to be commanded. Yes! Stop to actually LISTEN to God's orders to you.

♦♦ *If you move forward without heeding His commands, you walk alone.* ♦♦

Walking alone is not an option if we want to witness some Him-Possibly victorious finales in our lives!

Be blessed as you Pause today to receive your commands. *Then, move forward and watch the Him-Possible in action!*

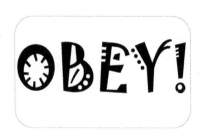

DAY 26-- Pause to Be Given (From God)

The most unhappy people in the world are takers. There's nothing satisfying about constantly wanting and demanding—and accepting—without reciprocating.

Instead, takers are dissatisfied, disgruntled, dysfunctional individuals who struggle with basic appreciation. Being thankful, showing gratitude; these are what balance out our human tendencies of selfishness and egotism--and takers lack these attributes.

All of us are receivers, whether we acknowledge that or not. But not all of us are takers. And not all of us are givers, either. The difference is not in the quantity of what is given to you, but in what you do with what you've received.

The GIVER is a receiver, too. But, the motive for their giving is NOT to receive, but to share something of value as a show of appreciation for what someone is or has done. All of us are receivers, whether we acknowledge that or not. But, not all of us are givers.

God is the foremost example of a GIVER, and His Word confirms this: "For God so loved the world, that He GAVE…" "He will GIVE you the desires of your heart." And, in today's scripture:

> • God has not given us a spirit of fear, but of power and of love and of a sound mind.
> ~2 Timothy 1:7 *(NKJV)*

- • God has GIVEN us a spirit of power.
- • He has GIVEN us a spirit of love.
- • He has GIVEN us a spirit of a sound mind.

And, it's what He has NOT given us that is so important in Trusting for the Him-Possible. ♦ *God has NOT given us the spirit of fear.* ♦ If you're fearing, you're Doubting. If you Doubt, you cannot trust. *Trusting implicitly, believing wholeheartedly, & having pure faith allow access to the*

Him-Possible! He modeled it to us, so that we might know the blessings of giving also.

> • Give, and it will be given to you: good measure, pressed down, shaken together, and running over will be put into your bosom. For with the same measure that you use, it will be measured back to you."
> ~Luke 6:38 *(NKJV)*

THE PAUSE

If you'll take the time to PAUSE for God to GIVE you —as a receiver, not as a taker—what He desires to Give, there will be NO room for Fear (Doubt)!! The difference is in your attitude. Believing you're worthy and entitled to any of God's gifts will make you a Taker. Humbly and graciously receiving God's gifts to you with gratefulness makes you a Receiver.

As a Receiver, your faith will increase and your trust in God's abilities will be multiplied. *Then the Him-Possible will be running over & spilling out of you.*

♦♦More blessings than you can contain.♦♦
More love. More power. More of a sound mind.

PRAYER & CONTEMPLATION:

Dearest Lord,
Today I am convicted. I sometimes have held back on graciously <u>receiving</u> due to a mistaken belief that I was being selfish and prideful. Instead, I find that if I only GIVE and fail to RECEIVE, I rob myself of opportunities to BE blessed, as well as to be a blessing! As contradictory as it seems, let me not allow a false sense of humility to keep me from receiving from You. Today, I <u>gratefully</u> receive whatever You choose to give! In Jesus' name, Amen.

DAY 27-- Pause to Receive a Promise

There is always that one child....

You know which one. (Maybe you ARE/WERE the one!) If it was declared to be impossible to climb that pole, scale that wall, jump that ditch, find that one lost piece, or fit one more cookie in its mouth — he/she would be The. One.

They're called, "strong-willed," "daring," "persistent," "stubborn," "headstrong," "defiant," and just plain ol' UNREASONABLE! But, the one thing they're NOT: Quitters!

You give them half a reason to figure out how to do something, and they'll do it. In fact, THEY'LL find the reason!

An even greater motivator for one of these people is to make them a promise, IF they can complete what "can't" be done. That promise can be a positive (reward) or a negative (punishment). Either one will do. They're out to achieve the impossible.

We love to read about & think of the myriad ways that God performed the impossible in the face of the naysayers. ◆*The more they said, "He CANNOT," the more God would prove He COULD!*◆

But, in today's account, we read the familiar story of Mary's visit from the angel announcing Jesus's miraculous conception and birth. Mary is <u>NOT</u> That. One. Child! *It appears she was content to live outside the 'bubble of challenge.'*

That's why the angel's announcement was even more disturbing to her serene, quiet, compliant nature. Her question wasn't one of stubborn resistance, or of needing to prove something. Instead, she wanted to understand WHY the Impossible was being presented for HER to accomplish.

- "Now indeed, Elizabeth your relative has also conceived a son in her old age; and this is now the sixth month for her who was called barren. For with God nothing will be impossible." Then Mary said, "Behold the maidservant of the Lord! Let it be to me according to your word." And the angel departed from her. ~Luke 1:36-38 *(NKJV)*

It seems the angel, Gabriel, was plenty glad to declare all the Impossible ways God was choosing to prove the Him-Possible! In fact, the statement, "For with God nothing will be impossible," is a declaration of fact AND faith by Gabriel.

Mary simply PAUSED and accepted the Promise given to her: "Let it be to me according to your word." She didn't make a spectacle of or draw unnecessary attention to herself. *She merely Paused and Accepted.*

And, THEN the Him-Possible occurred!!

◆◆ God's mission for this 'handmaiden of the Lord' was fulfilled NOT because she accepted a Challenge, but because she accepted a Promise! ◆◆

THE PAUSE

Today's Pause will require a great deal of restraint on your part. Our tendency is to second-guess or question something that is promised to us. We want to know what strings are attached, or what is required of us before receiving what we've been promised. We've been conditioned over time to believe that every promise comes with a stipulation.

Sometimes that is so. But, when God gives you a promise, your job is to accept it. *Without question, controversy, challenges, or confusion (Doubt), accept the promise.* Whatever situation you find presented to you today, you can see the Him-Possible transpire when you PAUSE and Accept the Promise first.

DAY 28-- Pause to Fine-Tune your Faith

One of the quirks about my late husband that I both admired and detested was his tendency to fine-tune things he would buy. Our viewpoints were opposite to one another on this. His philosophy was that anything could be made better with a little bit of tweaking. My philosophy is that it should be the way you want it when you purchase it, or don't purchase it at all!

I've watched car and lawn mower motors, hunting bows, radios, metal detectors, and guitars be worked on for hours —just to perfect one tiny thing. He believed it was already good, but that changing some small things would make it even better. So, he fine-tuned it.

Fine-tune = to make very small changes to something in order to make it work as well as possible: ~*Cambridge Dictionary*

Fine-tune =

a) to adjust precisely so as to bring to the highest level of performance or effectiveness

b) to improve through minor alteration or revision

~*Merriam-Webster Dictionary*

The act of fine-tuning sometimes requires that parts be removed, while other times, parts are added. The goal is to achieve that perfect balance between not enough and too much.

Our Faith is something that was already a part of us the day we surrendered to Christ. He purchased us with the belief that we would be a useful addition to His Kingdom. But, He also knew that our Faith could use some adjustments from time to time to make it better.

- But we all, with open face beholding as in a glass the glory of the Lord, are changed into

the same image from glory to glory, even as
by the Spirit of the Lord.

~2 Corinthians 3:1 *(KJV)*

Did you catch that? We should look in a 'spiritual mirror'
and see God's glory in us. BUT … we are also changed
(fine-tuned) from God's glory to God's glory. Not a
horizontal transformation, but a vertical moving up to
greater glory! In the following scripture, we can see that
our inward man is to be renewed day by day. Hmmmm.
That sounds to me a whole lot like it's being fine-tuned!

- For all things are for your sakes, that the
  abundant grace might through the
  thanksgiving of many redound to the glory of
  God. For which cause we faint not; but
  though our outward man perish, yet
  the inward man is renewed day by day. For
  our light affliction, which is but for a
  moment, worketh for us a far more
  exceeding and eternal weight of glory;

  ~2 Corinthians 4:15-17 *(KJV)*

In order for us to become exactly what God wants us to be, we have to be willing to endure some fine-tuning. We have to PAUSE to allow God to work on us. Changing into His image will take some chiseling to expose the beauty within. The closer we get to God by allowing Him free-reign with His tools, the more we will appear to be like Him! God will fine-tune what He sees — and make it better.

THE PAUSE

The daily renewal of our inward man — fine-tuning our spirits — allows our Faith to be turned over until we see it begin to work as it should. We already possess Faith, but our Faith can be fine-tuned to "work better."

Speak Life into situations you are facing. Do not allow any words of doubt or fear to inhabit your vocabulary. Listen to testimonies of others who have faced trials and who have overcome them victoriously. Do not forget: when we testify, we are usually on the OTHER side of a trial. So, many times, it may sound all rosy and great when we hear these testimonies. But, they came THROUGH it and have a testimony because of it. And, you will, too!

Faith produces miracles! ♦ *Fine-tuned Faith is Faith that does NOT doubt.* ♦ It is Faith that believes for the Him-Possible!

PRAYER & CONTEMPLATION:

God, let me always look at my Faith as having room for improvement! You've given me the ability to fine-tune it; to make it more effective, to work in various situations. Let me understand that You want me to be the best I can be for You and Your Kingdom. In order to do that, sometimes I need to add something to my faith – like virtue (moral excellence), and then knowledge, self-control, perseverance, and godliness, brotherly kindness, and love. Help me realize that my Faith, when it is perfected (brought to maturity), is a beautiful thing, and of better usefulness to You. In Jesus' name, Amen.

DAY 29-- Pause to Examine Scripture

When I was a teenager, I dubbed my step-mom the "Queen of Cliches," for her dozens (hundreds?) of daily adages. At that time, they annoyed me. Now, they fascinate me.

In fact, researching the origin of idioms is a fun hobby of mine. I find it very interesting to discern the derivation of certain phrases.

For instance, the phrase, 'Go through it with a fine-toothed comb,' means to "examine something scrupulously; to meticulously inspect, search with care, investigate."

It comes from the idea of searching the head for nits (lice), using a comb that would literally cover every strand—a fine-toothed comb. {That may be a little more information than some of you wanted to know, but you have to admit it is fascinating.}

Your walk with God and your Faith Walk in particular is too important not to give His instructions to us (the Bible) the consideration it deserves. When it comes to the Word of God, careful examination is not just a suggestion, it is vital.

- You search the Scriptures, for in them you think you have eternal life; and these are they which testify of Me."
  ~John 5:39 *(NKJV)*

Do you KNOW what you believe? Can you TESTIFY of Jesus—Who He was/is, Why He came to earth, What His mission was—and tell Where that information is located in Scripture?

God is not some genie in a lamp or fairy godmother that grants us wishes simply because we stumbled upon them. God is not a fairytale. *We believe firmly that HE is the ONLY God, and that we serve Him because of our confidence in that knowledge.* To know Him, then, is to

113

read His history, His biography, His story, and His love letters to us: the Bible.

THE PAUSE

These are ways we EXAMINE the Scriptures. We go over them with a fine-toothed comb, meticulously uncovering Truths. We investigate and inspect all aspects of Old Testament prophecy as it relates to the fulfillment in the New Testament.

We PAUSE to examine Scripture, so we may always give an answer.

> - But sanctify the Lord God in your hearts: and be ready always to give an answer to every man that asketh you a reason of the hope that is in you with meekness and fear:
> ~1 Peter 3:15 *(KJV)*

This Pause gives us confidence. Confidence that we know the only One who can truly do Him-Possible things—for us and for others.

DAY 30-- Pause to Turn Toward God

"Watch where you're going!" "Look out!" "Keep your eyes open!" "Pay attention!" "Watch your step!"

How many times have you admonished someone with you who was distracted? They might be wandering off the path, or getting too close to danger. They may have set their sights on something besides their destination. Their focus turned away, so their body followed.

> • Beware, brethren, lest there be in any of you
> an evil heart of unbelief in departing from
> the living God; ~Hebrews 3:12 *(NKJV)*

The use of the word, "beware" denotes a caution is being given; it is a warning to heed what follows. In this scripture, the admonition is to watch your heart—and the direction it might be headed!

Your heart will follow the direction of your focus. If you focus on faithfulness, your heart will be committed. If your gaze wanders to unstable pursuits, your heart will be fickle.

"An evil heart of unbelief" is not something we want to have. Yet, the possibility exists, or we would not have been warned about it. Unbelief in itself is not a good thing. The word indicates a lack of faith, a propensity to doubt, to question, to be skeptical. Those characteristics in a person will cause one not to believe in miracles, which is displeasing to God. The fact that a heart of unbelief was deemed 'evil' makes it even worse.

"Departing from the living God" is an exceedingly scary phrase. It means a person willfully changed directions. Their vision was no longer directed toward God, but began to Doubt.

Doubt arose—about God's goodness, the necessity of salvation, and His impending judgments. The "evil heart of unbelief" caused a turning AWAY from God. This would preclude the possibility of witnessing the miraculous. Because there is NO FAITH remaining.

THE PAUSE

Although this topic seems weighty, I'm glad that we have been presented with an avenue to redeem our path to the Him-Possible. Thankfully, God always provides a way to escape when we heed his warnings. In addressing the "beware," we see that the direction we head is up to us. *When we PAUSE to turn TOWARD God, our focus becomes more narrow, and our unbelief (Doubt) disappears.*

A narrow focus means clearer vision. We shut out things in our peripheral vision that distract us from our primary focus. Today, at the end of this series of devotions, let's Pause to turn our Focus to Faith.

♦ *A determination to leave Doubt behind makes way for the Him-Possible to occur!* ♦

Conclusion

Pausing. Stopping temporarily. Halting. Interrupting. Taking a break. What a revelation to know that sometimes God desires us to hesitate before jumping headlong into a spiritual battle. That's because He knows how important it is to observe the activity we are about to join, and to evaluate the best tactics for engaging. *That lull, that recess, that breather can make all the difference to the battle's outcome.*

During the writing of the original devotion from whence this book idea sprung, my family was faced with a serious health crisis. Although my faith was strong--due to the hours and hours of prayer and Biblical research I had undertaken to write the devotion--my faith was nevertheless challenged severely, seemingly overnight.

I believed for the Him-Possible to be done, and a miracle to take place. But--though I believed--God saw fit to answer in a different way. My life, as I knew it, was subsequently turned upside down, as a result.

While writing this book, distractions of all kinds, and sad news abounded. My faith was again challenged, but I knew that God COULD do the Him-Possible, IF that was His will. The enemy tried -- and he WILL try -- to discourage me and make me believe my words were ineffectual. He was unsuccessful. The finished book is proof of that!

But, my God is ABLE to do exceeding, abundantly ABOVE what I can ask or even think! I cling to that promise. My encouragement comes from BELIEVING that undeniable fact, without wavering.

I know that our finite minds can scarcely comprehend the infinite ways that God's answers are far superior to our own. My single prayer for you, the reader, is that these devotions have increased your Faith in ways you did not think could happen.

If you PAUSED each day to do what was instructed, you are now sitting in a place to watch the Him-Possible unfold before your faith-filled eyes! God bless you richly, and may your Faith continue to grow.

Acknowledgments

First of all, I give all honor to the ultimate Author--God, my Savior, Inspiration, and Friend. He gives the words. I am simply the Scribe.

Second, I wish to thank my late husband, Robert E. Hohman, Sr. for all his confidence in my abilities and his unwavering support of my talents. I only wish he was here to see the final result of his faith in me as a writer.

Thirdly, I can never say enough about my family—my 'kids,' who have always believed in me. They unceasingly prodded me to share thoughts, ideas, and stories via the written and spoken word because, "You have a voice that needs to be heard, Mom" they all said. I love you all so very much: Bobby & Amber Hohman, Heather & Corey Johnson, Haleigh & Jordan Arroyo, and Collin & Tiffany Hohman.

Next, to all my friends near and far who have believed in me for so, so long: this is the first of what I hope will be many books to come. You have cheered me on, and encouraged me to put the words in book form because, you said, "We want to be able to hold it, to re-read it, to have it in our hands."

Finally, I want to express my utmost gratefulness to Joyce & Kevin Hawkins, who provided a quiet space for me to finish this first endeavor. You'll never know what a blessing you truly gave me. And, to Pam Eddings, for her invaluable assistance in formatting and getting this book into print— thank you so much!

I appreciate all of you and know that without you, this would not have been possible.

~Susan

Author Bio:

Susan (Walton) Hohman has been writing for as long as she can remember. From the hand-written publication of a rural community newsletter, to serving on the journalism staff at her high school, to writing for various publications over the years, writing has been her passion, as well as her part-time vocation.

Married for over 33 years, and the mother of four adult children, she has long been prompted by her many friends and family members to publish a book. After the unexpected death of her husband, she found herself with time that was previously scheduled with duties as a pastor's wife, evangelist's wife, assistant pastor's wife, and home-schooling mother for over 22 years.

Now, with many more books started and in the process of being written, Susan's desire is to complete as many as she can, to make up for lost time! With any additional free time she now has, she travels to visit her children and grandchildren, who bring her great joy.

Susan's other interests include playing the piano, finding intriguing niche restaurants to explore, and researching and sharing trivial bits of information with anyone who will listen!

Made in the USA
Las Vegas, NV
09 September 2021